Arizona

impressions

FARCOUNTRY
PRESS

photography by Bernadette Heath and James Randklev

Right: Owl's clover, brittlebush, and ocotillo show their colors along Ajo Mountain Drive, Organ Pipe Cactus National Monument. JAMES RANDKLEV

Title page: Saguaro at sunset, Sierra Estrella Mountains in background. BERNADETTE HEATH

Front cover: Desert Viewpoint, Grand Canyon. JAMES RANDKLEV

Back cover: Manzanita line Long Canyon Trail, Maroon Mountain Range. BERNADETTE HEATH

ISBN: 156037-351-2
Photography © 2005 by Bernadette Heath and James Randklev
© 2005 Farcountry Press

For more information about our books write Farcountry Press, P.O. Box 5630, Helena, MT 59604; call (800) 821-3874; or visit www.farcountrypress.com.

Created, produced, and designed in the United States. Printed in China.

09 08 07 06 05 04   1 2 3 4 5

Above: The interior of Mission San Xavier del Bac, graced with ornate paintings, wood carvings, and statues, has been referred to as the "Sistine Chapel of North America." The depictions of more than 100 saints and 182 angels, as well as many murals, were cleaned and stabilized between 1992 and 1997. JAMES RANDKLEV

Facing page: Known as the "White Dove of the Desert," Mission San Xavier del Bac shimmers in the desert south of Tucson. The mission was founded in 1700 by Father Eusebio Francisco Kino, the "Padre on Horseback." Construction began in 1783 on this beautiful church, a blend of Moorish, Baroque, and Byzantine architecture that took fourteen years to complete. JAMES RANDKLEV

Right: Artesian wells make historic John Slaughter Ranch, along the Mexican border, a true oasis in the desert. Large stands of Fremont cottonwoods and several small ponds create a favorite stopover for migrating birds. Slaughter, a former Texas Ranger and cattleman, became Cochise County Sheriff and helped tame the infamous town of Tombstone. BERNADETTE HEATH

Below: Mescal Warm Springs in the Needles Eye Wilderness Area south of Globe is a remote riparian area. Here, columbines and ferns bordering the tiny creek hold back the Sonoran Desert terrain. BERNADETTE HEATH

Far left: A full moon reflects across Apache Lake's Mazatzal Bay in the Tonto National Forest. Horse Mesa Dam, one of a series of dams built along the Salt River, forms Apache Lake, a favorite fishing and boating destination for Phoenix residents. BERNADETTE HEATH

Left and below: La Placita Village is home to a colorful collection of offices, restaurants, and shops and the Pima County Sports Hall of Fame. The Metropolitan Tucson Convention and Visitors Bureau, also located here, offers maps for a self-guided walking tour of the plaza. JAMES RANDKLEV

Above: Globe roared into importance as a mining town in the 1870s. Silver drove the boom for four years, only to be replaced by copper mining. The town's historic district recalls the days when supplies had to be hauled by wagon from the nearest railroad 120 miles away. BERNADETTE HEATH

Right: The Mogollon Rim, often referred to as "the Rim," runs diagonally across the state, forming the southern ridge of the vast Colorado Plateau. Here, on Highway 260 between Heber and Payson, the 2,000-foot escarpment overlooks the Tonto Basin—site of the storied Graham-Tewksbury Feud in the 1880s. BERNADETTE HEATH

The Mittens, a classic of Monument Valley Navajo Tribal Park, were featured in many Western movies, including *The Searchers* starring John Wayne. Encompassing both sides of the Utah/Arizona border, Monument Valley's dramatic vistas have become a symbol of the Southwest. JAMES RANDKLEV

Facing page: Spanish conquistadors followed the Gila corridor to explore the Southwest. Early Native Americans farmed along the banks of the Gila, and today much of the river water is used for irrigation. BERNADETTE HEATH

Right and below: Phoenix's Heard Museum is described as "the nation's most prestigious private Indian arts center." The nonprofit museum was founded in 1929 to display Dwight B. and Maie Bartlett Heard's personal collection and is now one of the country's leading repositories for Native American art. JAMES RANDKLEV

Above: Tucson's historic district grew up around the Spanish presidio (fort). A walking tour, whether self-guided or the two-hour guided walk, shows off Tucson's Spanish roots. Most of the houses are built from adobe (mud bricks), the favored building material in a land short of timber. JAMES RANDKLEV

Facing Page: Tonto National Monument offers a high view of Roosevelt Lake. The monument features two cliff dwellings from the Salado culture. During spring, Mexican gold poppies provide a burst of color among the saguaros. JAMES RANDKLEV

Above: After crossing the Salt River, sheep move in a single line through Tonto National Forest. Two herders drive sheep to the White Mountains, which rise above 9,000 feet. In the fall, they retrace their long trek. BERNADETTE HEATH

Facing page: A replica of an old Spanish mission serves as the setting for many movies at Old Tucson Film Studios, which is open to the public. Guests can take rides, watch stunt scenes and gunfights, and learn about movie history. BERNADETTE HEATH

Right: Early morning light produces a surreal glow over Mount Hayden, as viewed from Point Imperial on the North Rim of Grand Canyon National Park. The North Rim receives 60 percent more moisture than the more heavily visited South Rim, which is more than 1,000 feet lower. The North Rim is closed from early fall to mid-May because of snow. JAMES RANDKLEV

Below: Cholla cactus blossoms show their colors in Organ Pipe Cactus National Monument. There are twenty-eight different species of cholla in Arizona, all bristling with spines. JAMES RANDKLEV

Left: Cathedral Peaks at Red Rock Crossing, Sedona, is a favorite of photographers. Tiny Oak Creek eroded the sandstone buttes from ancient sand dunes. In late October, trees along Oak Creek display stunning red and gold hues. JAMES RANDKLEV

Below: Nathan's Bridge in Hewitt Canyon hides in the Superstition Mountain Wilderness Area. The mountains, rumored to be home to the fabled Lost Dutchman Gold Mine, are a hodgepodge of steep canyons, volcanic plugs, and eroded mountains. BERNADETTE HEATH

Above: A collared lizard suns itself along the Peralta Trail in the Superstition Mountains. Because they are cold-blooded, lizards must "sun" on rocks in the morning to warm up then hide in shady crooks and crannies during daytime to prevent overheating. BERNADETTE HEATH

Right: Unlike most Arizona rivers, Canyon Creek runs from west to east through the Fort Apache Reservation. Ancient ancestral Puebloan sites are secreted away in rugged canyons. Theories like drought, overpopulation, and warfare attempt to explain the disappearance of these early Native Americans around A.D. 1300. BERNADETTE HEATH

Facing page: Angels Window, at the Grand Canyon, was formed by wind and water, the same erosional forces that created the canyon itself. Far in the background loom the snow-covered tops of the San Francisco Peaks, the highest mountains in Arizona. BERNADETTE HEATH

Left: Petrified Forest National Park is strewn with stone tree trunks from the Triassic Period. JAMES RANDKLEV

Below: Marble Canyon is the official start of the Grand Canyon and the entry point for adventurous rafters. John Wesley Powell, famous Grand Canyon explorer, named this canyon. When he looked up at these majestic cliffs from his tiny wooden boat, he thought they were marble. BERNADETTE HEATH

Right: Organ Pipe Cactus National Monument along the Mexico border is extremely hot in the summer but a favorite spot for winter visitors. The organ pipe cactus is named as such because its arms grow close together at the ground then spread upward, resembling the pipes of an organ. JAMES RANDKLEV

Below: According to the tower clock on the Second Pinal County Courthouse at Florence, it is always 9 o'clock. The clock has never run because the funds for a working clock were used to build a jail. The citizens felt a jail was needed much more than the correct time. BERNADETTE HEATH

Facing page: Red sandstone cliffs are signature features of the Navajo Reservation. In the northeastern corner of the state near the Chuska Mountains, the cliffs seem to glow at sunset. The multi-colored clay at the base of the cliffs is knows as the Chinle Formation and can be found in the Painted Desert and other colorful areas of northern Arizona. BERNADETTE HEATH

Right: Justin Heaton takes time to pet his dog, Scrappy, after a long day in the saddle. The Heaton family has ranched on the remote Arizona Strip for four generations. Familar with the country, Justin also leads horseback rides into the nearby Kanab Creek Wilderness Area bordering Grand Canyon National Park. BERNADETTE HEATH

Below: Range horses graze knee-deep in grass near the Santa Rita Mountains, Coronado National Forest. The lush grasslands along the Santa Cruz River attracted early cattlemen. Today, mesquite trees compete with the grass for precious water. BERNADETTE HEATH

Above: When Hoover Dam was completed in 1935, it was the largest dam in the world. Built for electricity and flood control on the Colorado River, it is more than sixty stories high and backs up Lake Mead, the largest manmade lake in the Western Hemisphere. Originally called Boulder Dam, the name was changed to Hoover Dam, back to Boulder Dam, and then back again to Hoover Dam—following the whims of politics. LAURENCE PARENT

Right: London Bridge, "the world's largest antique," spans a channel at Lake Havasu City. In the 1960s, Robert McCulloch paid $2,460,000 for the London Bridge and another $7 million to transport the 10,276 granite blocks from London and rebuild the structure at Lake Havasu City. STEPHEN TRIMBLE

Left: The Chiricahua National Monument, along the New Mexico border in southern Arizona, is known as a "wonderland of rocks." Twenty-five million years ago, an immense volcanic explosion sent ash flows careening down the slopes. When the flow stopped, the ash was so hot that it fused into rock known as "welded tuff." This tuff eroded into the maze of strange columns, spires, and hoodoos that became the hideout for the Chiricahua Apaches and their leader, Cochise. LAURENCE PARENT

Below: Aloe vera and poppies bloom and the oblong pads of prickly pear cactus stand against an aged wooden fence. Prickly pear cactus is common throughout Arizona. The red fruit of the cactus is eaten by wildlife and people alike; prickly pear jelly is sold in many gift shops. JAMES RANDKLEV

Above: Herrera House in Tubac Presidio State Historical Park reflects typical Southwest Spanish style. Set along the Santa Cruz River with a backdrop of the Santa Rita Mountains, today Tubac is a thriving artists colony offering a variety of interesting shops. BERNADETTE HEATH

Right: The towers of downtown Phoenix, as seen here from the Arizona Center, give dramatic proof of the city's fast growth. Water channeled from the Salt River turned the desert around Phoenix into productive agricultural lands, which then gave rise to the development of the bustling metropolis. Centuries before, Hohokam Indians used canals to divert water from the Salt and Gila rivers to irrigate their crops. BERNADETTE HEATH

Right: Spectacular storm clouds hang over Sedona's red rock country. This photo, taken from Bear Mountain, gives a haunting glimpse of light and shadow on the famous buttes and cliffs. BERNADETTE HEATH

Below: A tourist boat plies Lake Mead along the Nevada border. Formed by Hoover Dam, this 100-mile lake starts in rugged Black Canyon. The white line around the edge is the high-water mark and is commonly called the "bathtub ring." LAURENCE PARENT

Above: A gentle mourning dove sits on her nest protected by the spines of a staghorn cactus. The bird's name comes from the soft, cooing sounds it makes. Many animals have found security among thorny cacti. JAMES RANDKLEV

Facing page: At 9,157 feet, Mount Lemmon north of Tucson boasts the southernmost ski resort in the United States. Here, fresh snowfall lies undisturbed among the stately ponderosa pines. JAMES RANDKLEV

Above: The Desert Botanical Garden in Phoenix contains 145 acres of red rock buttes and more than 20,000 desert plants. Both visitors and residents enjoy paths that meander through one of the world's most well-maintained gardens. Renowned for its cactus collection, it contains desert plants from all over the world. JAMES RANDKLEV

Facing page: The old Camp Reno Road passed across this saguaro-covered plain near the rugged McDowell Mountains. During the Apache Wars, soldiers from Fort McDowell, located at the juncture of Sycamore Creek and the Verde River, made the exhausting journey to Camp Reno near present-day Roosevelt Lake. BERNADETTE HEATH

Above: A bull rider tries to hold on for his eight seconds of glory at the Tucson Rodeo. La Fiesta de los Vaqueros is an annual event celebrating Tucson's Old West heritage. JAMES RANDKLEV

Left: The Aztec House of Antiques is fronted by old saddles and wagon wheels reminiscent of the heyday of Tombstone, the "Town Too Tough to Die." When prospector Ed Schieffelin searched for gold and silver in southeastern Arizona, skeptics predicted all he would find in the hostile land would be his own tombstone. When he made a rich silver strike, he called his mine the Tombstone. BERNADETTE HEATH

Above: Grapevine Creek and the roots of an alder tree in the Prescott National Forest make a spot for peaceful meditation. BERNADETTE HEATH

Right: Roper Lake reflects the beauty of 10,713-foot Mount Graham. Roper Lake State Park near Safford not only offers camping, fishing, and bird watching, but it has a public, outdoor hot tub fed by one of the many warm springs in the region. BERNADETTE HEATH

Above: The old storefront of the Elysian Grove Market is guarded by prickly pear cactus. A walk through Tucson's historic Barrio District reveals more buildings from the town's colorful Spanish period. JAMES RANDKLEV

Left: San Tan Mountain Regional Park southeast of Phoenix near Queen Creek showcases the Sonoran Desert. Here a saguaro cactus displays its "arms." The largest cactus in the Southwest, saguaros grow so slowly that arm buds usually don't appear until the plants are 75 to 100 years old. After rainfall, the accordion-like pleats on the trunk expand as the saguaro draws up water from its shallow roots. BERNADETTE HEATH

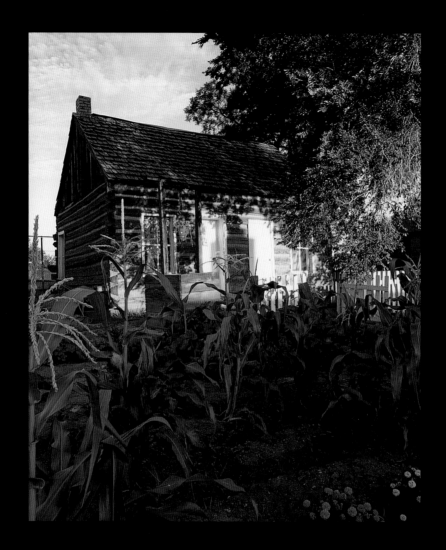

Above: In St. Johns' historic museum, a rebuilt log cabin sits on the edge of a cornfield. Built along the banks of the Little Colorado River, St. Johns was first settled in the early 1870s by Mexican families and later by Mormon settlers. BERNADETTE HEATH

Facing page: Sunlight reflects on serene Oak Creek at Slide Rock State Park. This gentle creek is responsible for carving much of the famous red rock formations near Sedona. Slide Rock State Park, with its natural chutes and swimming holes, is a popular spot to escape hot summer days. JAMES RANDKLEV

Above: Although it is open year round, the 7,000-foot elevation of the South Rim of the Grand Canyon means it receives snow during winter. Down at the bottom of the gorge, the weather is similar to that of Phoenix. Shown here is the top rock layer of the Grand Canyon, Kaibab limestone. These rocks were laid down 250 million years ago. JAMES RANDKLEV

Facing page: A monument to the Navajo Code Talkers is displayed in Phoenix. During World War II, 375 to 420 Navajo Marines transmitted military information in their native language; the Japanese military never broke the code. The Navajos' valuable service was instrumental in many of the Pacific campaigns, including the battle for Iwo Jima. JAMES RANDKLEV

Facing page: Aspens frame snow-capped San Francisco Peak in Coconino National Forest.
JAMES RANDKLEV

Below: A coyote pup peeks out of its den in the San Tan Mountains. A mother coyote usually gives birth to a litter of six pups, which she keeps hidden in an underground den while she hunts for food. Coyotes have adapted well to humans and are found throughout the state.
BERNADETTE HEATH

Right: Sedona's elite Tlaquepaque Plaza holds dozens of shops offering paintings, sculptures, weavings, and more. Sedona, named for a woman settler, has evolved from a simple agricultural community to a Mecca for artists. Native American petroglyphs and pictographs, some thousands of years old, decorate the sheer red walls. JAMES RANDKLEV

Below: La Fiesta de los Vaqueros Parade, Tucson. JAMES RANDKLEV

Facing page: At twilight, the lights of downtown Tucson illuminate a city that has seen slow and steady change. From its beginnings as a Native American village along the Santa Cruz River in A.D. 800, Tucson has grown to a modern metropolitan area proud of its history. JAMES RANDKLEV

Below: These yellow blooms appear on prickly pear cactus between April and June. This photograph was taken in Saguaro National Park near Tucson. The park, divided into two sections—Saguaro East, at the foot of the Rincon Mountains, and Saguaro West, backed up against the Tucson Mountains—is a favorite place for many to enjoy springtime flower displays. JAMES RANDKLEV

Above: The Verde River starts on the slopes of the Mogollon Rim and winds its way southeast to join the Salt River north of Phoenix. Here the river cuts through rocky terrain just below Horseshoe Dam. This dam, the uppermost dam on the Verde, was built for flood control in the 1940s. BERNADETTE HEATH

Facing Page: Sedona homes enjoy spectacular views of the red-and-white cliffs. A popular way to experience red rock country is by hiking or mountain biking. Trails in the Munds Mountain, Red Rock-Secret Canyon, and Sycamore Canyon wilderness areas near Sedona afford views of vermilion mesas, canyons, and buttes. JAMES RANDKLEV

Above: Fall colors of gold and orange cling to white-limbed sycamore trees in Sabino Canyon in the Catalina Mountains north of Tucson. A shuttle tram takes visitors up the scenic canyon to enjoy hiking, swimming, picnicking, and birding. JAMES RANDKLEV

Right: A young Navajo girl in traditional dress sits in Monument Valley Navajo Tribal Park. Navajos still graze their sheep in this sparse high desert of the Colorado Plateau. JAMES RANDKLEV

Facing page: Graceful Havasu Falls, in the Grand Canyon, drops nearly 200 feet to the turquoise pool below. JAMES RANDKLEV

Right: Blooming brittlebush and owl's clover brighten hillsides along Ajo Mountain Drive at Organ Pipe Cactus National Monument. JAMES RANDKLEV

Below: Mountain biking is popular along Arizona's many backcountry trails. Here, at Star Pass in the West Tucson Mountains, bikers enjoy a spring day in the desert. JAMES RANDKLEV

Above: Petroglyphs at Signal Mountain, Saguaro National Park. Saguaro National Park near Tucson is divided into eastern and western sections. Along the Signal Hill Petroglyph Trail in the western section, petroglyphs etched into stone are evidence of the Hohokams, a tribe that vanished around A.D. 1450. JAMES RANDKLEV

Left: One of the most popular places to view the Grand Canyon is from Mather Point on the South Rim. At 7,120 feet in elevation, the buttes, towers, and labyrinth of canyons that make up the Grand Canyon spread in a glorious panorama. Here, the wild geology of the Southwest is displayed in colorful strata. JAMES RANDKLEV

Above: The guard tower still dominates the Yuma Territorial Prison State Historical Park. About 3,000 men and 29 women were confined here during the prison's 33 years of operation. It closed in 1909. BERNADETTE HEATH

Left: Sunrise on Lake Powell showcases loco weed, yucca, and evening primrose near Gunsight Butte. Formed by Glen Canyon Dam, Lake Powell has 1,960 miles of shoreline. BERNADETTE HEATH

Above: Kartchner Caverns State Park is the crown jewel of Arizona's state park system. Located between Benson and Sierra Vista in southeastern Arizona, Kartchner Caverns is a wet, living cave in which calcium carbonate features are still growing. Humidity is high—98 percent—in the 58-degree cave. Maybe you will be lucky enough to feel a droplet of water hit you—called "cave kisses," these droplets are rumored to bring good fortune.
BERNADETTE HEATH

Right: The two-tailed swallowtail is Arizona's state butterfly. Growing up to five inches in length, it has two tails on the bottom of each wing. BERNADETTE HEATH

Facing Page: Sabino Canyon, springtime brings verdant growth in this lush canyon of the Catalinas near Tucson.
JAMES RANDKLEV

Above: Winter sun warms a cliff dwelling in Montezuma Castle National Monument. Built by the Sinagua culture around A.D. 1250, this twenty-room site took advantage of solar heating in the winter. The limestone overhang provided shade, as well as protection from rain and snow. BERNADETTE HEATH

Facing page: Sun highlights the Grand Falls on the Navajo Nation. The majestic falls only appear when the Little Colorado River floods. BERNADETTE HEATH

Facing page: The White Mountains in far eastern Arizona offer a respite from the summer desert heat. Formed by ancient volcanoes, this region is home to the White Mountain Apache tribe, which holds 11,490-foot Mt. Baldy sacred. In the winter, skiers enjoy the tribe's Sunrise Ski Area. BERNADETTE HEATH

Below: After a wet winter, Mexican gold poppies blanket the rugged slopes of Picacho Peak State Park. Composed of volcanic rock, Picacho Peak has long been a desert landmark and was the site of small Civil War battle. JAMES RANDKLEV

Facing page: Rancho de la Osa (Ranch of the She-Bear) sits along the Mexican border near Sasabe. The thick-walled adobe ranch house is now a bed-and-breakfast furnished with Spanish antiques. BERNADETTE HEATH

Below: Sunrise casts the Coyote Buttes in Vermilion Cliffs in soft morning light. Layered and swirled by wind and water, Coyote Buttes is one of the most spectacular settings in a region known for beautiful rock formations. BERNADETTE HEATH

Above: The Apache Maid Ranch in Coconino National Forest was a thriving cattle ranch in the late 1800s. The ranch was a popular stopover for travelers going from northern Arizona to Camp Verde along the Verde River. BERNADETTE HEATH

Left: Bits and bridles hang on the wall at a ranch along the Blue River. Surrounded by the Blue Range Primitive Area, this area along the Arizona/New Mexico border is one of the most remote regions in the state. BERNADETTE HEATH

Facing page: Cowboy lifestyle is still going strong in Arizona. Here a cowboy ropes a steer in the Tonto National Forest. BERNADETTE HEATH

BERNADETTE HEATH. Multimedia artist Bernadette Heath brings to photography her experience in many other aspects of the art world. Using nature as her model, she first created with pen and ink, watercolor, clay, and glass. When she moved to the Southwest, it seemed natural for her to pick up a camera and hike off into the mountains. Working with light, forms, shadows, color, people, animals, and passion are all the elements in fine art.

Heath's photographs have been published in *Arizona Highways Magazine, National Geographic, National Geographic Adventure, Cerca Magazine, Audubon, National Wildlife Federation, American Forests, AAA Highroads,* and *Elle Decor Magazine.* Her work has also appeared in books published by the Western National Park Association, Arizona Highways, Rio Nuevo Publishers, Farcountry Press, Newbridge Publishing, McRae Books Srl, Madden Publishing, and Starlight Publishing. Heath has received awards from the National Federation of Press Women and the SATW Bill Muster Photo Showcase. www.BernadetteHeath.com

JAMES RANDKLEV. Master landscape photographer James Randklev has photographed America for thirty years, primarily with a large-format camera that provides the rich images collected in this volume. His brilliant and sensitive work has made him one of the Sierra Club's most published photographers. His color photographs have appeared in books, periodicals, calendars, and advertising—and they have been exhibited in shows in the United States and abroad. In 1997 he was the sole American chosen to exhibit in the International Exhibition of Nature Photography in Evian, France. In 2003 Randklev was selected to be included a book entitled *World's Top Landscape Photographers—and the Stories Behind Their Greatest Images* by Roto Vision Publications, London, England. Randklev's photography books include *In Nature's Heart: The Wilderness Days of John Muir; Georgia: Images of Wildness; Wild and Scenic Florida; Georgia Impressions; Georgia Simply Beautiful; Olympic National Park Impressions; Florida Impressions; Florida Simply Beautiful;* and *Bryce Canyon National Park Impressions.*

www.JamesRandklev.com

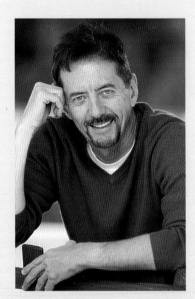